DATE DUE			

CHARLES BURTON MARSHALL

AMERICAN FOREIGN POLICY
AS A DIMENSION
OF THE AMERICAN REVOLUTION

Distinguished Lecture Series
on
the Bicentennial

This lecture is one in a series sponsored
by the American Enterprise Institute
in celebration of the Bicentennial of the United States.
The views expressed are those of the lecturers
and do not necessarily reflect
the views of the staff, officers or trustees of AEI.
All of the lectures in this series will be
collected later in a single volume.

revolution · continuity · promise

CHARLES BURTON MARSHALL

AMERICAN FOREIGN POLICY
AS A DIMENSION
OF THE AMERICAN REVOLUTION

Delivered in
the Benjamin Franklin Room, Department of State
Washington, D. C.
on
May 22, 1974

American Enterprise Institute for Public Policy Research
Washington, D. C.

© 1974 by American Enterprise Institute
for Public Policy Research, Washington, D. C.

ISBN 0-8447-1315-5

Library of Congress Catalog Card Number L.C. 74-83419

Printed in the United States of America

In early May of 1774 the ship *Lively* brought to Boston details of the British Parliament's response to the Boston Tea Party, five months past. Boston was to be devitalized—stripped of status as a colonial capital, its customs house removed, its commerce interdicted. The news spread posthaste and, by this time of the month 200 years ago, was known from New Hampshire to Georgia. Through a dire spring and summer, retribution would be compounded. Massachusetts would be reduced to a royal satrapy—its colonial charter rescinded, elections and town meetings deauthorized, quartering of troops on municipalities reinstituted, and venue shifted to the Crown's advantage in criminal cases linked to civil resistance. Parliament in London—in unison with an adamant King George III—meant business. To work their will, both would not scruple about overturning any recalcitrant colony's internal arrangements. Such was the sense conveyed by the actions.

Those events of 1774 are recalled for commemorative sentiment in part but also, and more to the point, for their significance in great developments pertinent to our topic. They marked a stage in what John Adams called "the real American Revolution" —a revolution not to be pinpointed in time. It was a revolution, as John Adams said, "effected before the war commenced" and consisting of a "radical change in the principles, opinions, sentiments, and affections of the people." [1] The recounted events sig-

---

[1] Charles Francis Adams, ed., *The Works of John Adams* (Boston: Little, Brown & Co., 1856), vol. 10, p. 262.

naled a beginning to the end of illusions under which the restive colonists had been pressing their grievances. As one sees in retrospect, though the point was not yet apparent to the colonists, the spring and summer of 1774 prefigured eventual and inevitable repudiation of British rule—the Revolution registered and explained to "a candid World" in the Declaration of Independence on July 4 two years later.

The Declaration—in which the enduring name of our polity was coined—serves as a main frame of reference for this discourse. I shall take account also of some ideas incident to that antecedent Revolution stressed by John Adams. For perspective, it is fitting to touch briefly on the character of a long, complicated quarrel between Britain and colonial America.

I remember having sworn allegiance to the United States of America in eleven oaths, each taken without any mental reservation whatsoever. I make that point in hope of forestalling any wrong inference from what I am about to say. In making ready for this occasion, I sometimes wondered where my sympathies might have lain at various stages—with the resisters, with London's partisans, or with the uncommitted—if I had been on the colonial scene during the fifteen years of intensifying strife preceding the Declaration of Independence. Because no twentieth-century person can determine his answers to eighteenth-century questions, obviously what I asked was fanciful and vain, but I asked it anyway.

In my imagined answer, considerations of practicality would have aligned me with the alienated colonists. London—too remote —was implausible as a seat of authority for the thirteen dissident colonies. Edmund Burke put the matter cogently in Parliament:

> Three thousand miles of ocean lie between you and them.
> No contrivance can prevent the effect of this distance
> in weakening government. Seas roll, and months pass,
> between the order and the execution; and the want of a
> speedy explanation of a single point is enough to defeat
> a whole system.[2]

Decision makers in London—even though not as folly-prone or as tyrannous as portrayed in patriot agitation—did, in their ignorance

---

[2] Ross J. S. Hoffman and Paul Levack, eds., *Burke's Politics: Selected Writings and Speeches of Edmund Burke on Reform, Revolution, and War* (New York: Alfred A. Knopf, Inc., 1949), p. 72.

2

of America, demonstrate Burke's further observation about incompatibility between great empire and small minds.[3] The constraining of American production and trade to British mercantilist practices would have seemed anomalous and unacceptable—the weightiest consideration of all.

Whatever their tacit views, colonial militants did not articulate their case on such pragmatic grounds. They argued mainly from abstract constitutional principles. The nub of their case—"no taxation without representation"—had more lilt than logic. The proposition begged more questions than it clarified.[4] The counter case put by such loyalists as Martin Howard, Samuel Seabury, Joseph Galloway, and Daniel Leonard, though less romantically expressed, had some good points.

The intricate events of 1761 to 1776, all well known and needing no retelling, were rooted in a British constitutional background dating to a distant past when all governing powers, undifferentiated in kind, had belonged unequivocally to the monarch. By imperceptible stages over centuries, royal power had been hedged about by the obliging of kings to take counsel from ministers of wise repute before making decisions, by widening the circle of counselors on periodic occasions to include besides a king's ministers the realm's secular and ecclesiastical lords and some portion of men of prominence chosen by election in their localities, by sorting such summoned advisers into two houses of Parliament whose joint approval became a condition precedent to extensions of royal power into new patterns of action within the realm, and by requiring affirmation by the elected house—the House of Commons—in the authorizing of taxes.

In the long process of bridling kings, developments of the middle and latter 1600s are especially relevant. The epoch seethed over the question of what, if any, powers remained to the king's and his ministers' discretion and, in contrast, what powers had become subject to parliamentary sanction and direction. Issues about the apportionment of power between a conceptual king-in-Parliament and a conceptual king-out-of-Parliament entailed, as

---

[3] Ibid., p. 94.

[4] Howard Mumford Jones, *Revolution and Romanticism* (Cambridge: Harvard University Press, 1974), p. 189.

we know, two revolutions and cost two monarchs their crowns and one his head. Momentum was with Parliament. The upshot in 1688 registered parliamentary supremacy as an accomplished fact. Victory went to the Whig side and against the Tories, as Parliament's and the king's factions were known. Thenceforth an omnipotent Parliament's sufferance would determine what prerogatives kings might retain.

The effects on linkage between Britain and the transatlantic colonies, all of them established by authorizations and initiatives involving exercise of royal prerogative pure and simple, are what concern us here. After proving Charles I's dispensability at the chopping block, the Long Parliament (actually a rump of the House of Commons acting alone in the enforced absence of the House of Lords) established a commonwealth to be governed "by the Supreme Authority of this Nation, The Representatives of the People in Parliament, and by such as they shall appoint and constitute as Officers and Ministers" and to engross "the People of England, and of the Dominions and Territories thereunto belonging." The kingless commonwealth proved transient, but the innovative subordination to Parliament of territories beyond the realm was reaffirmed in the oath prescribed by Parliament in 1688 for the investiture of William and Mary following the cashiering of James II.

The gist of that required pledge to govern the kingdom "and the Dominions thereunto belonging according to the Statutes in Parliament agreed on" was unequivocal. Colonies were adjuncts to the realm. The link of empire inhered in Parliament. Parliament's paramountcy within the realm encompassed the adjuncts. A king's subordination to Parliament applied beyond as well as within the realm. His subjects wherever located came within Parliament's jurisdiction. Whatever immunities might have been granted in previous exercises of prerogative were revocable privileges and could not possibly foreclose the supreme Parliament's power over the colonies.

By a contrary postulate, the Crown provided empire's link. A king's subservience to Parliament within the realm did not apply beyond. His kingship in New York, Massachusetts, Virginia, and the rest was no mere derivation from his status within Britain. The colonies, however subject to Parliament's will in externalities, were beyond its reach in internal matters—an exemption constituting an irrevocable right. A subject of the king abiding in the colonies could not be bound by Parliament. Parliament's assertion of a self-expanding jurisdiction was invalid. Such in simple essence were the premises underlying colonial resistance when, eventually, it developed.

The roots of confrontation lay in a multiplicity of circumstances, but the clash, when it came, was rationalized in terms of the two irreconcilable sets of constitutional propositions. The word "constitution" and what it meant were, as Bernard Bailyn has observed, centrally important to the colonists' position:

> . . . their entire understanding of the crisis . . . rested upon it. So strategically located was this idea in the minds of both English and Americans, and so great was the pressure placed upon it . . . that in the end it was forced apart, along the seam of a basic ambiguity, to form the two contrasting concepts of constitutionalism that have remained characteristic of England and America ever since.[5]

Theoretically—a point made by Charles Howard McIlwain a half-century ago[6]—the American rebellion might be backdated to 1649. In fact, the clash remained latent and revolutionary resistance was out of mind, so long as Parliament's asserted supremacy over and within the colonies was only declaratory and ritual. The occasion for division and the stimulus of rebellion grew out of the Seven Years' War and the operative changes which it brought to the British governing role in America.

The eighteenth century's most pervasive conflict entailed large deployments of British forces to save the colonies from extinction. The mother country's power became as never before a palpable presence on the American scene. The operations of war incurred great expense. Constitutional theorizing aside, a sharing of the resulting financial burden was not unreasonable, and the portion allocated to the colonies was equitable. Should

---

[5] Bernard Bailyn, *The Ideological Origins of the American Revolution* (Cambridge: Harvard University Press, 1967), p. 67.

[6] Charles Howard McIlwain, *The American Revolution: A Constitutional Interpretation* (New York: Macmillan Co., 1923), p. 9.

the king's subjects everywhere get the benefits but only those in Britain pay the bill for security? Tax resisters answered first with an elusive distinction between external taxes and internal—the one sort legitimately assessable, the second wholly unacceptable—and then with a denial altogether of Parliament's authority to levy taxes.

Both sides seem to have argued from misplaced tradition. Each strove for something new in a guise of vindicating something established—the British for an imperial commonwealth centrally dominated as never before except in ritual forms, the resisters for a league of equals beyond experience and even beyond their articulation. As Randolph G. Adams has written—

> America, after the French and Indian War, was a nation which had outgrown its old political garments. To its clamor for new institutions, necessary to fit the new conditions, the restrictive policy of the old colonial system brought more swaddling clothes.[7]

In an ironical reversal of arguments of a sort recurrent in politics, it fell to successive Parliaments preponderantly of Tory stripe, and to a king of similar outlook, to apply, in trying to enforce taxation within America, the Whig postulate of Parliament's pervasive supremacy. The tax resisters, Whig in persuasion and adopted name, relied on old Tory themes of royal prerogative. No diminution of prerogative was wished, as the Continental Congress—assembled to coordinate resistance in face of the coercive actions of 1774—sought to assure George III. That "best of Kings," as he was called, was inaccessible to arguments based on distinction between kingly office and parliamentary scope. For the time being, tension between throne and Parliament was minimal. In form the king was subservient to a parliamentary majority, while in substance dominating it through manipulative patronage.

Four years later resistance would make its point. George III would declare "fit for Bedlam" anyone upholding taxation of America. Besides retreating on taxes, Britain would offer the colonies representation in Parliament and promise amnesty for rebellion. It would be too late, for by then the fighting begun in

---

[7] Randolph G. Adams, *Political Ideas of the American Revolution,* 3d ed. (New York: Barnes & Noble, 1958), p. 38.

6

1775 as constitutional resistance to assertedly unconstitutional acts had become, as perhaps it had to become, irreversibly a revolutionary war, and the rebelling colonists had contracted with Britain's inveterate enemy, France, to persevere until British acknowledgment of the independence of the United States of America.

II

A proper juncture at which to date the shift from constitutional resistance to revolution would be May 15, 1776. On that day the successor Continental Congress, calling them states, summoned the colonies to "take up government" and to suppress in their territories all exercise of authority under the Crown. A more explicit resolution of independence was passed by the Congress approximately seven weeks later, on July 2, to be followed two days later by adoption of the Declaration, traditionally cited as marking the onset of the Revolution.

Constitutional logic, fine points about ancient usages, citations of institutional precedent, and the like were no longer relevant. The issue with the mother country was not susceptible of adjustment. The outcome would be determined by factors of will and raw power. Abridging the well-worn arguments of the preceding fifteen years, the Declaration adduced a different line of reasoning for a new situation. Its terms provided the rational foundation for war.

What constitutes war is worth a moment's consideration. First, war is a conflict of purposes, initially considered irreconcilable, between two sides consisting of states or organized societies akin to states to the extent at least of having or aspiring for exclusive control over spans of territory, possessing schemes of authority for directing general affairs, and disposing aggregates of persons—armed forces—organized for transmitting energy and discharging it with destructive intent against enemy armed forces and other resources serviceable for waging war. Second, in war, so as to make the conflicted purposes reconcilable on terms to its own advantage, each side strives for a radical shift in relative capability, measured in the moral factor of will or in material factors or both, for persevering. Third, in war, the two sides must actually employ their armed forces against each other.

Wars vary expansively or contractively as determined by interacting dimensions implicit in the definition given—war aims, the degree of their mutual irreconcilability, numbers and magnitudes of participants, importance and inclinations of those standing aside, strength and unity and authority and civil will on the opposing sides, the size of their armed forces and other resources for inflicting destruction, levels of diversion of resources from civil enjoyment to uses of war, theaters of hostilities, rates of destruction wrought, and duration. Every war must end. Any war will end when both sides prefer the terms available for closing it to the perceived effects of continuing it. Successful conduct of war entails handling its interrelated aspects so as to ensure that the adversary side shall be the one compelled to scale down its aims so as to get the war over with.

The standard ingredients of war were already at hand in mid-1776. The Declaration illuminated rather than established that circumstance. It defined the issue at stake—not a mere matter of tax jurisdiction, constitutional procedure, or proper allocation of authority, but the prizes of statehood and sovereignty. The Americans assumed "among the Powers of the Earth" a "separate and equal Station." No longer would London be the determiner and medium of their relations with the great globe. They claimed "full power to levy War, conclude Peace, contract Alliances, establish Commerce, and to do all other Acts and Things which Independent States may of right do." The vicarious, inequalitarian devices of empire must be ended. In their own way and own right, the Americans thenceforth must participate in the nexus of diplomacy—a word, by the way, not yet in usage at the time and therefore, obviously, not explicitly in the Declaration. To acquiesce in a settlement of the war providing anything less would amount to defeat.

The Declaration was an exercise in psychological warfare, though the key word "psychological" had not yet entered the language. As such, it aimed for preemption of the moral high ground in hope thereby of generating resolution on the patriot side, rallying support wherever else possible, and contributing to

8

discomposing civil will within the adversary establishment. Terms of sublime innocence were chosen to depict every premise, interest, purpose, and mode of conduct on the patriot side. The Declaration contrived "to conjure . . . a vision of the virtuous and long suffering colonists standing like martyrs to receive on their defenseless heads the ceaseless blows of the tyrant's hand." [8] The "British Brethren" were appealed to in the name of "their native Justice and Magnanimity" and "the Ties of our common Kindred." With a bill of twenty-eight accusatory particulars, which took up about half of its 1,337 words, the document portrayed George III—so recently "the best of Kings"—as an agent of "Cruelty and Perfidy, scarcely paralleled in the most barbarous Ages, and totally unworthy of the Head of a civilized Nation" and as "A Prince, whose Character is thus marked by every Act which may define a Tyrant, . . . unfit to be the Ruler of a free People." Hitler in the dock at Nuremberg could scarcely have been more vigorously arraigned.

The Declaration—a more important point—was a bid to make victory a plausible outcome by attracting allies and encouraging a benign tilt on the part of governments standing aside as neutrals. These aims went hand in hand with the aspiration for independence. Without drawing in allies, the aspirants could scarcely expect to escape the eventuality of having to settle for an accommodation within the British system. For any purpose less than detachment from the Crown, with corollary effects of damaging British power and prestige and of opening up market opportunities through abolishing Britain's monopolistic control over their external commerce, the Americans could scarcely hope to induce third-party interposition by Britain's strategic rivals or even benevolence from Britain's competitors in trade.

Beyond making a case for severing old political associations and for making war, the Declaration also articulated an array of assumptions and precepts concerning the nature, norms, and values of political existence. In these respects, too, it had—and still has— a bearing on international affairs, though that word "international" was not in the text, for indeed in 1776 the word was still a dozen years short of invention.

---

[8] Carl Lotus Becker, *The Declaration of Independence* (New York: Harcourt, Brace, 1922) , p. 207.

Rufus Choate called the Declaration a collection of "glittering and sounding generalities." [9] In Gilbert Chinard's appraisal of a half-century ago the Declaration—with its "sentences so balanced and so rythmic that no artist in style could improve upon them"—rated as "the first and to this day the most outstanding monument in American literature." [10] John Adams once likened the Declaration to "a juvenile declamation." [11] Late in life, Thomas Jefferson, the principal author, found "heavenly comfort" in its abiding appeal to his countrymen, whereas Timothy Pickering, a reluctant third in the succession of United States secretaries of state, wished it to be consigned "to utter oblivion" for its polemical excesses.[12]

On balance, the ayes have it. Moses Tyler's estimate written in the late nineteenth century is a representative judgment. Jefferson, he said

> gathered up the thoughts and emotions and even the characteristic phrases of the people for whom he wrote, and these he perfectly incorporated with what was already in his own mind, and then to the music of his own keen, rich, passionate and enkindling style, he mustered them into that stately and triumphant procession wherein, as some of us still think, they will go marching on to the world's end.[13]

Amid the redundant triviality of contemporary political discourse one reads the document with envy for a time when statesmanship was capable of elegant language and knew how to unite history with literature.

Jefferson "turned to neither book nor pamphlet" while drafting the Declaration. That is what he said—and we should believe him—in recalling the rush job a half-century later. He named Aristotle, Cicero, John Locke, and Algernon Sidney as sources

---

[9] Quoted in Samuel Gilman Brown, *The Life of Rufus Choate* (Boston: Little, Brown & Co., 1898), p. 326.

[10] Gilbert Chinard, *Thomas Jefferson: The Apostle of Americanism* (Boston: Little, Brown & Co., 1939), p. 72.

[11] Quoted in Edward Dumbauld, *The Declaration of Independence* (Norman: University of Oklahoma Press, 1950), p. 14.

[12] Quoted in Jones, *Revolution and Romanticism,* p. 161.

[13] Moses Coit Tyler, *The Literary History of the American Revolution, 1763-1783* (New York: Putnam, 1847), vol. 1, p. 508.

10

of ideas in his mind, adding an "etc." to the list.[14] Expositors who have analyzed the text with a thoroughness befitting exegetes of Holy Writ have found hints of the Baron de Montesquieu, Jean Jacques Rousseau, James Wilson, George Mason, Tom Paine, and dozens more in its nuances. Jefferson surely had read them all. His "sensitized mind picked up and transmitted every novel vibration in the intellectual air."[15] Jefferson had internalized that great age's multifarious literature of reason, felicity, harmony of interest, moral order, natural liberty, progress, and vaulting confidence in the clarity of moral principles and in making new starts. The Declaration—resonant with ideas from the Enlightenment—was, and is, "a characteristic product of the *saeculum rationalisticum*" representing, according to Michael Oakeshott, "the politics of the felt need interpreted with the aid of an ideology."[16]

Conceivably, the claim of independence could have been based on simple pragmatic considerations. The outworn British imperial system simply was not working. To have the Americans out rather than in would be better for all concerned. Such a case invoking practical particulars would not have been in the style of the times. Instead, to provide moral and legal justification, the argument must be founded on universal abstractions—unalienable rights and the Law of Nature and of Nature's God—of a sort entailing vagueness. The focus was self-determination. The main reliance was on a concept of social contract derived from Locke's late seventeenth-century Whig theory that perceived government as an instrument to ensure people's preexisting rights and preconceived purposes, empowered by people's consent only for those ends and subject to overturn for failing or exceeding them. The case to be made must be large enough to engross all humanity. Conjectural premises were mentioned as truths held to be self-evident. We think them; therefore they are so! More forthright Cartesian self-assertiveness would be hard to imagine.

The United States Constitution, then still a dozen years in the offing, would be of a different order. The national leadership

---

[14] Chinard, *Thomas Jefferson: The Apostle of Americanism,* pp. 71-72.

[15] Carl Becker, *The Heavenly City of the Eighteenth Century Philosophers* (New Haven: Yale University Press, 1932), p. 34.

[16] Michael Oakeshott, *Rationalism in Politics* (London: Methuen & Co., Ltd., 1962), p. 28.

echoed in the Constitution would have become less hortatory. The content would show recognition of a need for more than abstract good ideas in order to maintain a nation as a going concern. An important lesson regarding linkage between independence and capacity and will to meet obligations would be mirrored. To keep attuned to a supposed harmony of interest was not enough. The nation must put itself in position to attend to its own concerns more effectively. No language implying a world mission would be offered. The Constitution would be intent on perfecting the union of states. It would be concerned with justice within—justice not as a spontaneous abstraction, but justice as a function of authority. The tranquility asserted as an aim would be domestic tranquility. The common defense to be worked at would pertain to security for a national base. The welfare postulated as an end for policy would be that of the generality of Americans. Liberty's blessings would be coveted for "ourselves and our posterity." Domestic concerns they all would be.

Of the two founding documents, the Declaration—forming part of the poetry, as distinguished from the logic, of politics—has proved to be the one of greater affective appeal for the conduct of foreign policy. As Dexter Perkins has observed, "American statesmen have believed, and have acted on the belief, that the best way to rally American opinion behind their purposes is to assert a moral principle. In doing so, they have often gone beyond the boundaries of expediency."[17] The Declaration has offered a ready catalogue of relevant apothegms and analogies. The practice of invoking them has not been a matter of mere rhetoric or propaganda, of humoring preconceptions, or of guessing what will go over with the public. Ideas explicit or implicit in the Declaration have endured as legitimizing concepts in the national psyche. Presidents, their spokesmen, and their principal advisers have been wont to turn to such ideas as a way of validating policy undertakings in their own minds. Thus, in a manner unparalleled, our twentieth-century conduct in world affairs has been accounted for in eighteenth-century frames of thought. Similarly, a proclivity for "massive stereotypes" and "galloping abstractions"—in Charles

---

[17] Dexter Perkins, *The United States and Latin America* (Baton Rouge: Louisiana State University Press, 1961), p. 19.

Frankel's terms[18]—has been stimulated within what are known as intellectual circles.

Yet little analysis on international politics and foreign relations is to be found in the Declaration. The lack is consistent with Locke's philosophy, which, though full of ideas about harnessing government domestically, recognized the great role of contingency in the handling of externals:

> But what is to be done in reference to foreigners depending much upon their actions, and the variation of designs and interests, must be left in great part to the prudence of those who have this power committed to them, to be managed by the best of their skill for the advantage of the commonwealth.[19]

The pertinence of the Declaration inheres mainly in the fact that the nation came into existence on the basis of a concept of self-determination asserted to be universally applicable. That concept itself could scarcely be said to have been subject to much analysis.

The "fateful document," as an Englishman once remarked, contained, if not the death sentence, then at least the epitaph of empire.[20] Self-determination has become the political absolute of our time—a development for which the American instance has served as precedent if not cause. The concept, ambiguous at the moment of origin, remains so still. The Declaration uttered the notion as a justification for war and a condition of peace, as a claim to national autonomy and as an invitation to intervention. When Woodrow Wilson at Versailles invoked self-determination as a basis for universal peace-making, his secretary of state, Robert Lansing, warned that he was establishing a rationale for innumerable wars to come.[21] It was a prophetic judgment. Both sides in every conflict since World War II, as I recall, have championed the idea. Its ambiguity, as between an interventionist and a non-

---

[18] Charles Frankel, "The Scribblers and International Relations," *Foreign Affairs* (October 1965), p. 2.

[19] John Locke, *Of Civil Government* (New York: E. P. Dutton & Co., 1924), pp. 191-192.

[20] William Thomas Stead, *The Americanisation of the World, or the Trend of the Twentieth Century* (London: Markley, 1901), p. 32.

[21] Robert Lansing, *The Peace Negotiations: A Personal Narrative* (New York: Houghton Mifflin Co., 1921), pp. 93-108.

interventionist doctrine, has perhaps never been better demonstrated than it was, unconsciously, by the late President Lyndon Johnson in his State of the Union Message eight years ago. He described "support of national independence—the right of each people to govern themselves and to shape their own institutions" as "the most important principle of our foreign policy." He added: "For a peaceful world order will be possible only when each country walks the way that it has chosen to walk itself." Then he summed up: "We follow this principle abroad . . . by continued hostility to the rule of the many by the few." [22]

A few auxiliary elements of the Declaration may also be cited, for an analytic reader might wish for more prescient care in the wording of some of the aphorisms. For example, I wish more explication had been supplied for the key word "rights" invoked in support of a number of desiderata. Something said by Oswald Spengler is pertinent: "Rights result from obligations. An obligation is the right of another against me." [23] I am skeptical of a tendency, prevalent in our times, to apply the word as a label for every preference in national or international affairs, for where every goal becomes expressible as a right, then the extent and tightness of the pattern of obligation become total, grace and its counterpart, gratitude, are obviated, and civil existence takes on a tribal sort of rigidity.   ·

I wish Jefferson had rethought his stipulation of "Life, Liberty, and the Pursuit of Happiness" as natural rights. As Justice Oliver Wendell Holmes observed, "The most fundamental of the supposed preexisting rights—the right to life—is sacrificed without a scruple not only in war, but whenever the interest of society, that is, of the predominant power in the community, is thought to demand it." [24] Every law abridges liberty. As for the pursuit of happiness, was realization or merely endless quest assured? Was happiness meant in the sense of good luck, pleasure, or spiritual composure? Whatever the meaning, the word in a context of natural rights is anomalous. Here, too, Spengler is

---

[22] *Department of State Bulletin,* January 31, 1966, p. 152.

[23] Oswald Spengler, *Aphorisms* (Chicago: Henry Regnery Co., 1967), p. 122.

[24] Oliver Wendell Holmes, *Collected Legal Papers* (New York: Harcourt, Brace, 1920), p. 304.

relevant: "Happiness is unexpected, rare, unlikely, brief and blindly appreciated. The less men have brooded about the nature of happiness, or their right to it, the happier they have been." [25]

I should like to have some exposition of the word "equal" in a clause alleging the condition into which all men—meaning a species rather than a gender—are created. In logic such a term needs a referent. Equal in what specific respects? Equality in civil capacity, presumably, was intended. Yet that thought seems contradicted by a later reference to "merciless savage Indians," for how could so invidious a phrase have been used if all were civilly equal? The text does not articulate a distinction between equality as "a concept for dealing out justice between incommensurable human beings"—to use Jacques Barzun's apt phrase [26]—and equality taken as a circumstance bestowed by nature so that any demonstrable disparity becomes proof of deviancy and injustice. I wish also the document had been more precise about linkage between equality and liberty, both terms occurring in the same sentence. Obviously, in logic, neither abstraction can be considered absolute in coexistence with the other. The tension between them—later so perceptively examined by Alexis de Tocqueville—was not even hinted at in the Declaration.[27]

My last such point concerns an appeal in the Declaration for support among people of informed judgment in certain other lands. Jefferson dressed the idea in words about "a decent Respect to the Opinions of Mankind." Today's etiquette would require "person-kind," but I shall let that point pass. A significant shade of distinction obtains between judgment and opinion. "Mankind" in such a context is a phantom notion. In Spengler's words again: " 'Mankind' has no more goal, purpose, or plan than the species butterfly or orchid. 'Mankind' is either a zoological concept or an empty word." [28] The phrase in the Declaration humors illusions of finding wisdom in amorphous aggregates and contributes to a fallacy—if I may quote the late Dean Acheson—of feeling obligated

---

[25] Spengler, *Aphorisms,* p. 40.

[26] Jacques Barzun, *Darwin, Marx, Wagner* (Garden City: Doubleday & Co., Inc., 1958) , p. 360.

[27] Alexis de Tocqueville, *Democracy in America* (New York: Schocken Books, Inc., 1961), vol. 2, pp. 113-117.

[28] Spengler, *Aphorisms,* p. 46.

to turn on a wind machine because others are whipping up a cyclone. I deplore it, as I deplore the other loose phrases, for encouragement given to sentimentality in international affairs.

Woodrow Wilson's effort to get the United States into the League of Nations, which he conceived as "the organized opinion of mankind," [29] was a relatively recent event when, forty-four years ago, I first took undergraduate courses in international relations and foreign policy. The few textbooks available were all innocent of conspiracy, espionage, propaganda, subversion, states' propensities for leading double lives, and other "political phenomena that are ubiquitous, though universally condemned." [30] The complexity of institutions called governments and the multifarious interplay between domestic forces and external affairs were scarcely mentioned. Rationalism, in Michael Oakeshott's sense of the term, dominated the portrayal. International relations were seen as a high-minded enterprise wanting only enhanced commitments to community, candor, and cooperation in order for permanent world tranquility to be achieved. Disarmament, popular control of governments, and public education were main avenues to that end. The chief impeding circumstance was accounted to be the United States' lamented default on President Wilson's design for applying the principles of the Declaration of Independence worldwide—a dereliction needing to be redressed by participation and commitment, whereupon the momentum toward world cooperation would gain irresistible momentum.

Having low regard for the assignments, I saved myself from complete obfuscation about the world's prospects by reading such unprescribed items as spy stories, science fiction, and accounts of

[29] Ray Stannard Baker and William S. Dodd, *War and Peace: Presidential Messages, Addresses, and Public Papers (1917-1924) by Woodrow Wilson* (New York: Harper & Row, 1927), p. 234.

[30] Carl J. Friedrich, *The Pathology of Politics* (New York: Harper & Row, 1972), p. 1.

wars to come in the Sunday newspaper supplements and certain sensational magazines. Within a few years my reading choice would be vindicated. Soon afterwards, the United States would reverse its habits, become an inveterate participant, thereupon contract a multiplicity of international strategic responsibilities borne at fabulous expense, and find itself involved in fifteen intermittent years of distant hostilities. The great undertakings during three-and-a-half decades of unprecedented activity in world affairs—the Atlantic Charter, lend-lease, the forming of the grand coalition in World War II, the reincarnated Wilsonian dream of a world organization, the Truman Doctrine, the Marshall Plan, innumerable economic development programs, a global array of alliances, and two Asian wars—have all been executed in declared fealty to principles enunciated in the Declaration of Independence.

I do not need to relate the details of those great efforts, or to labor the recent changes in national mood. General states of mind are politically significant in themselves. The simple fact of wide concurrence on the reality of a shift in the conditions of international politics is self-validating evidence. The disposition now prevailing is to shrug off notions about being guardians of global security, exemplars and nurturers of innumerable other societies' livelihoods and civil morale, and preceptors to an array of fatalistic peoples on how to shape their destinies.

Something deeper than fatigue and discomfiture growing out of the Vietnam experience seems to be involved. In successive seminars in recent years I have had my students, as one assignment, scan the Declaration, single out the postulates, precepts, and nuances bearing on the nature of public life and the good of the state, and see what ones they accept as plausible. In surprising proportions, the students prove never to have read the document before, profess to find it fascinating, but express skepticism about the assumptions and expectations reflected in it. It is not necessary to go so far back to find a point of reference for making a modest test of altered mood. A similar process applied to President John F. Kennedy's inaugural address, so impressive to so many for its elan and affirmativeness only thirteen years ago, has produced similar responses: "Let every nation know, whether it wishes us well or ill, that we shall pay any price, bear any burden, meet any hardship, support any friend, oppose any foe to assure the survival and the success of liberty."[31] To some of my students that utterance, so boundless, was as if from another century.

One discerns here a retreat from certainty—a phenomenon which Allen Wheelis ponders in *The End of the Modern Age*. "At the beginning of the Modern Age," Wheelis writes, "science did, indeed, promise certainty. It does no longer."[32] Sir John Squire has expressed the same thought. He quotes from Alexander Pope:

> Nature and Nature's laws lay hid in night:
> God said "Let Newton be!" and all was light.

He adds:

> It did not last: the Devil howling "Ho,
> Let Einstein be," restored the status quo.[33]

Wheelis sums up the difference. "Certainty," he says, "leads us to attack evil; being less sure we would but resist it."

My closing remarks are personal observations appropriate for a time of doubt. I do not share the current mood of ennui and discouragement. I have never participated in vaulting hopes for the finite, fallible aspect of existence called policy. As far back as I can remember I would have concurred with Herbert Butterfield's thought:

> And . . . we have been particularly spoiled; for the men of the Old Testament, the ancient Greeks and all our ancestors down to the seventeenth century betray in their philosophy and their outlook a terrible awareness of the chanciness of human life, and the precarious nature of man's existence in this risky universe. These things— though they are part of the fundamental experience of mankind—have been greatly concealed from recent generations because modern science and organization enabled us to build up such a tremendous barrier against fire, famine, plague and violence. The modern world created so vast a system of insurance against the contingencies and

---

[31] *Department of State Bulletin*, February 6, 1961, p. 175.

[32] Allen Wheelis, *The End of the Modern Age* (New York: Basic Books, Inc., 1972) , p. 114.

[33] John Collins Squire, *Collected Poems* (London: Macmillan Co., 1959) , p. 210.

18

accidents of time, that we imagined all the risk eliminated—imagined that it was normal to have a smooth going-on, and that the uncertainties of life in the past had been due to mere inefficiency.[34]

Uncertainties inherent in policy do not put me off.

> For nothing worthy proving can be proven,
> Nor yet disproven. Wherefore thou be wise,
> Cleave ever to the sunnier side of doubt.[35]

Like Othello, I can say, "I have done the state some service." He could add, ". . . and they know't." Mine was obscure. From it I shall call up one recollection. At a serious juncture back in Truman times I was over at the White House to help in the drafting of a grave presidential message to Congress. The President's counsel said the President desired to have in it some passages about the light at the end of the tunnel. I made a skeptical comment. The counsel inquired what I expected to find at the end of the tunnel. I answered, "Another tunnel, of course." I remember that interchange because the former counsel, encountered at a social occasion recently, recalled it with an observation, "How right you were!"

In that spirit—had I been alive in the United States' formative years—I probably would have regarded the more buoyant asseverations in the Declaration as skeptically as, in my own time, I have regarded the promising frills with which magistrates are wont to embellish their initiatives in foreign policy. Rather than Jeffersonian enthusiasms, I fancy I would have shared—along with his grasp of the essence of independence and his love for country—John Adams' pessimism as it developed in his later years.[36]

The essence of the Declaration was, and is, in the phrase about assuming "among the Powers of the Earth the separate and equal Station." The heart of the Declaration—the action parts—concerned power. A commendable chapter in Professor Bailyn's book

---

[34] Herbert Butterfield, *Christianity and History* (New York: Charles Scribner's Sons, 1950) , pp. 69-70.

[35] Alfred Lord Tennyson, *Complete Poetical Works* (Boston: Houghton Mifflin Co., 1898) , p. 498.

[36] John R. Howe, Jr., *The Changing Political Thought of John Adams* (Princeton: Princeton University Press, 1966) , pp. 102-132.

on *The Ideological Origins of the American Revolution* [37] delineates the colonists' anxieties about "the endlessly propulsive tendency" of power. Albeit, they "had no doubt about what power was and about its central dynamic role in any political system." Power was what the colonists sought and what they used, intrepidly, in the seeking. I stress the point because one hears in these times so much vain counsel to the nation about perils of power and the wisdom of shedding it.

Thrice in recent months I have heard Lord Acton's famous aphorism about power invoked—and inevitably misquoted—in support of such notions. Acton's apothegm was once given its proper rating as a "legend . . . best attributed to that instinctive piety which leads men to denigrate what they dearly cherish." [38] I trouble to consider it only to rebut certain false corollaries. The phrase is not, "Power corrupts." It is, "Power tends to corrupt"— to which Acton added, "and absolute power corrupts absolutely." [39] True, power can be misused. Possessors of it may mistake means for ends, abandon perspective, and end up done in by their own instruments. What is fallacious is implicitly to associate such perversion exclusively with power.

Courage can be distorted into foolhardiness, pride into pridefulness, thrift into greed, generosity into improvidence, trust into gullibility, faithfulness into folly, humility into supineness, and charity into degradation. No virtue is immune to vice. Shakespeare wrote of a man destroyed by too possessive a love. Goethe wrote of a man put in eternal peril by excessive thirst for knowledge. Hardy portrayed a man undone by overweening desire to be right. Kipling told of a man who self-destructively overdid the very idea of not overdoing. An entity that would renounce faculties because they involve moral risk can only end up as a moral cipher. The corollary of "power tends to corrupt" is not that loss of power redeems. A master-slave relationship is morally destructive to the slave as to the master.

---

[37] Bailyn, *Ideological Origins,* pp. 55-93.

[38] Lord Radcliffe, *The Problem of Power* (London: Martin, Secker & Warburg, 1952) , p. 4.

[39] Hugh A. MacDougall, ed., *Lord Acton on Papal Power* (London: Sheed and Ward, 1973) , p. 230.

20

Sovereignty—a word not in the text, perhaps because the Americans associated it explicitly with repudiated British rule [40]— also sums up the goal of the Declaration, though whether it was sought for one or for thirteen components was unclear. How many times over the years have I heard someone in an audience, using a tone of discovery, suggest abandonment of sovereignty so as to abolish danger and achieve concord! Sovereignty is merely an abstract expression for a finite government's possession of resources and faculties for coping. It comes from having a scheme of authority capable of maintaining dependable social order, command of the allegiance of a determining portion of the populace encompassed, and common recollections and expectations sufficient to form a bond of identity among that portion. Sovereignty comes also from a conscious general purpose to amount to something significant in the world's annals, from capacity and will to command means and to devote them to realizing common preferences and to enter into and effectuate external obligations, from capability to affect environing conditions as well as to be affected by them, and from a system of agency able to represent the realm by communicating authentically and conclusively on its behalf to others beyond its span. Which of these would any sound person wish the nation to give up? These faculties and qualities are hard to come by. They are not a fixed reality, not an inherent endowment. We would forfeit any of them at peril. If we ever lose them, we can only say, quoting Spengler, "World politics destroys those countries that are not up to it." [41]

My final thought is about love of country. On a speaking occasion a few years ago, I was charged by a certain publisher in the audience with advocating a principle of "my country right or wrong." I did not deny it. I demurred. The authentic words of the Stephen Decatur aphorism are: "Our country, in her intercourse with other nations, may she always be in the right, but, right or wrong, our country!" The first part is Decatur's prayer for national perfection. The second comes to terms with the human situation. As I told the reproachful publisher, I might say the same thing for my family—wishing my children perfect, but

---

[40] Bailyn, *Ideological Origins*, p. 229.
[41] Spengler, *Aphorisms*, p. 120.

knowing they will not be, will err, and will get into trouble. When that happens, should I renounce them? No. Should I do otherwise for the society of whose institutions I have been beneficiary and for the land which is the scene of my best recollections? Moreover, one must recognize the elements of tragedy in the human situation. The import of tragedy is that human beings and human institutions may get done in for their virtues as well as by their vices. Any tragedy which befalls this society, this state, this government—all of them finite, contingent, and fallible—will not spare me. So it is my country, right or wrong.

Cover and book design: Pat Taylor

The Department of State
harbors a number of official reception rooms. The largest,
an appropriate setting for a foreign policy lecture,
is the Benjamin Franklin State Dining Room.

Pamphlets in AEI's Distinguished Lecture Series on the Bicentennial of the United States, 1973-74

- **Irving Kristol**
  The American Revolution as a Successful Revolution

- **Martin Diamond**
  The Revolution of Sober Expectations

- **Paul G. Kauper**
  The Higher Law and the Rights of Man in a Revolutionary Society

- **Robert A. Nisbet**
  The Social Impact of the Revolution

- **Gordon Stewart Wood**
  Revolution and the Political Integration of the Enslaved and Disenfranchised

- **Caroline Robbins**
  The Pursuit of Happiness

- **Peter L. Berger**
  Religion in a Revolutionary Society

- **G. Warren Nutter**
  Freedom in a Revolutionary Economy

- **Vermont Royster**
  The American Press and the Revolutionary Tradition

- **Edward C. Banfield**
  The City and the Revolutionary Tradition

  Leo Marx
  The American Revolution and the American Landscape

  Ronald S. Berman
  Intellect and Education in a Revolutionary Society

  Kenneth B. Clark
  The American Revolution: Democratic Politics and Popular Education

  Seymour Martin Lipset
  Opportunity and Welfare in the First New Nation

  Forrest Carlisle Pogue
  The Revolutionary Transformation of the Art of War

- **Charles Burton Marshall**
  American Foreign Policy as a Dimension of the American Revolution

  Dean Rusk
  The American Revolution and the Future

- *Now available in print at $1.00 each.*